WIN YOUR RACE

Matthew Awujoola

Win Your Race
Copyright ©2021 by Matthew O. Awujoola
All rights reserved. No portion of this publication may be used without the express written consent of the publisher.

Published by

Quickword Edge
Lagos, Nigeria

09053744043; 08033517205
quickwordedge.info@gmail.com
1Akinsanya Street, Somolu,
Lagos, Nigeria

For further enquires, contact
Matthew O. Awujoola
LAGOS EAST BAPTIST CONFERENCE SECRETARIAT,
Baptist Academy Compound, Obanikoro, Lagos
matthewawujoola@hotmail.co.uk
09053744043; 08033517205

All Bible quotations are taken from The Holy Bible: New International Version. Copyright © 1973, 1978, 1984, by International Bible Society

Acknowledgment

When you are blessed with the most important gift on earth, the gift of people, you are truly blessed in indeed in life. With the gift of good people, you cannot but succeed. I am bold to say I am blessed with great people.

This book is dedicated to the entire Kingdom People of Lagos East Baptist Conference. Your fervent support for the advancement of God's kingdom is highly appreciated and may it be abundantly rewarded.

I also acknowledge the works of some authors and speakers whose message might have filtered through my thought in this book. Thank you for your labour of love to the advancement of humanity.

Golden Texts

However, I consider my life worth nothing to me; my only aim is to finish the race and complete the task the Lord Jesus has given me —the task of testifying to the good news of God's grace.
(Acts 20:24 NIV)

*I'm not there yet, nor have I become perfect; but I am charging on to gain anything and everything the Anointed One, Jesus, has in store for me—and nothing will stand in my way because He has grabbed me and won't let me go.
Brothers and sisters, as I said, I know I have not arrived; but there's one thing I am doing: I'm leaving my old life behind, putting everything on the line for this mission. I am sprinting toward the only goal that counts: to cross the line, to win the prize, and to hear God's call to resurrection life found exclusively in Jesus the Anointed.
All of us who are mature ought to think the same way about these matters. If you have a different attitude, then*

God will reveal this to you as well. For now, let's hold on to what we have been shown and keep in step with these teachings.
(Philippians 3:12-16 The Voice)

Contents

Acknowledgment 5
Chapter 1 9
Chapter 2 13
Chapter 3 21
Chapter 3 26
Chapter 4 28
Chapter 5 34

Chapter 1

INTRODUCTION: Your Life Journey Is Like a Race

> "It's your road and yours alone, others may walk it with you,
> but no one can walk it for you."
> - **Anonymous**

There was a dramatic experience at the Athens' 2004 Olympic in the men's marathon. During the race, a runner, Vanderiel Cordeiro de Lime, who was leading with reasonable margin was suddenly obstructed by an intruder from the crowd. Vanderiel was pushed off the course and delayed for few minutes that made others to bypass him. Initially he was emotionally and physically disturbed by this unexpected disruption for few minutes. He, however, continued the race. He adjusted and recovered mentally again. Thank goodness, he kept running, forging ahead with all his strength and ended the race in third place, winning the bronze medal.

The Christian life is a race so also is life. Both started at a point, we face all kinds of hurdles as we steadily move towards immediate and ultimate awards, trophies and ultimately the end. Paul the Apostle, recognising the significance of his Christian journey and life assignments, asserts: "However, I consider my life worth nothing to me; my only aim is to finish the race and complete the task the Lord Jesus has given me —the task of testifying to the good news of God's grace." (Acts 20:24 NIV). The race is so precious that Paul was ready to give it whatever it takes to end well and joyfully.

We shall consider our theme in three dimensions:
- The need to discover the race;
- The need to be intentional about the race and
- The need to go for the gold, winning the race by removing impediments to ending your race with joy.

It does not matter how long one lives on earth, he will leave one day. It is pertinent therefore, to live well with two greatest impressions. One is to use this season of existence to impact the people well, leaving a legacy of positive impact. The second is to use this journey of life to prepare for the life after death. Both the impact we made on people and the relationship we had with Jesus Christ will matter greatly whether we ended well our race while here on earth or not.

INTERACTIVE SESSION

Chapter 1: Your Life Is Like a Race

1. Can you mention some of the things people live for that you think is wrong?

   _____
   _____
   _____
   _____
   _____
   _____
   _____
   _____
   _____
   _____

2. Why do you think the above reasons do not worth living for?

   _____
   _____
   _____
   _____
   _____
   _____
   _____
   _____
   _____
   _____

3. What does living to make positive impact on others mean to you?

   _____
   _____
   _____
   _____

_____
_____
_____
_____
_____
_____

4. In your own words describe what it means to have a relationship with God?

_____
_____
_____
_____
_____
_____
_____
_____

5. Mention three major ways you are practically impacting people.

   a. _____
   _____

   b. _____
   _____

   c. _____
   _____

Chapter 2
KNOW YOUR RACE

"Your life isn't an accident.
You have a destiny, one that only you can complete."
– Rick Warren

In 2017 the world fastest sprinter declared after his retirement that he would be going into professional football. He was so keen about becoming a professional soccer player and he went for it despite skepticism from several quarters. Everyone who heard him, felt how will such a strong as wind sprinter, with such a huge unbeatable record, succeeds as a footballer?

Not minding the distractions and side comments Bolt believed he had the speed as well as the required talent to play football successfully as a professional. He began his football career by training with some clubs in Europe. Good enough for him he was featured in some competitions and made remarkable impression of the possibility of realizing his dream as a footballer.

Record has it that in 2018 Usain Bolt made great attempt at enlisting himself on the scoresheet during some marches. Especially in 2019 he scored a goal in one of the competitions and had himself on the scoresheet. However, things did not work as projected for him. Reasons why he could not further his dreams are blamed on few points. Apart from the fact that the negotiation price never worked with some clubs trying to engage him some other factors worked against him.

It is generally believed that Bolt failed because he lacked the required basic football intelligence and not fit enough to last for the required basic duration of ninety minutes for football marches. The rule is different. Usain Bolt is good for race of nine minutes, but not with ninety. He must stay with his race.

As human beings we all, are wonderfully and fearfully made (Psalm 139:14), but wonderfully made differently. We are unique in various ways. The power of identity has proven to us that no two persons, even the so-called identical twins, are the same. In God's technology our temperament, genetic construction, physiological makeup, fingerprints and other things classify individuals as unique entities. This uniqueness also manifests in our desires, aspirations, giftings, talents, career and calling.

The Bible is filled with examples of people who became successful and end well because they discovered and walked *within their race in life*. What does this mean? For example, in I Corinthians 3:6, Paul identified himself as planter and Apollos as he that waters with respect to functioning in building the Corinthian church. Similarly, Paul in Galatians 2:7 gave a clear understanding of his calling as an apostle to the Gentiles while Peter, another major leader, as an apostle to the Jews. It is discovered that those who have succeeded in their careers and callings are those who have a clear understanding of what they are here on earth for.

How do I know my race? This is the probing question in the heart of many, especially the young ones. The first way to know your race in life is to go back to God who made you. The best way to know the purpose or function of a product is by reading and understanding the manufacturer's manual. God made us, "Know that the LORD is God.It is he who made us, and we are his; we are his people, the sheep of his pasture." (Psalm 100:3 NIV). When you sincerely ask God, He will guide you through His Spirit and discerning people to know what you are made for.

The second way to know is also by making yourself vulnerable. To be vulnerable is to expose yourself to things that exposes your weaknesses and strength without being ashamed. You become vulnerable by becoming available for service. What a footballer can do is best known when he submits to a coach during training. Availability for service of all kinds helps you to discover your best area of functioning. Try your hands on many things that you have interest in. People call it "trial and error", we call it exploration. In this process you will fail, make mistakes, stumble and this is painful and shameful but at the end of the day you will succeed.

Those who truly understand their race, will equally have a good knowledge of the requirements of running the race effectively.

> Do you not know that in a race all the runners run, but only one gets the prize? Run in such a way as to get the prize. Everyone who competes in the games goes into strict training. They do it to get a crown that will not last, but we do it to get a crown that will last forever. Therefore I do

not run like someone running aimlessly; I do not fight like a boxer beating the air. No, I strike a blow to my body and make it my slave so that after I have preached to others, I myself will not be disqualified for the prize. (I Cor. 9:24-27 NIV).

The picture here, in the passage, is that winning the race requires some qualities or qualifications: The first is discipline. It takes a lot of energy, practice and tenacity to compete well with others and possibly win. Competition or the ancient Olympic like what we have today is beyond mere entertainment. A lot of background rehearsals and funds go into it to prepare the competitors for the games. When the contestant deprives himself enough of those enticing foods, pleasure and leisure he will surely excel and joyfully receive the crown.

The second requirement is observation of the applicable rules. Rules are instructions guiding the race. The instructions contain dos and don'ts that the contestants must adhere to before and during the race. When contestants fail to observe these rules, they risk disqualification and all those periods of discipline is wasted, the crown and the joy of competing is missed.

In the third place, those who know what they are set for will learn to pay the price for the race. No race without its attending pains. People who know what they are called for are ready to pay the price. Without paying the price, there can be no prize. Some of the prices include discouragement, temptations that tempt their integrity, and sometimes too, early celebration of achievement.

One major beauty of knowing one's task is that it helps one to get direction. It helps one to know where to exert one's energy on. At this point no beating about the bush again. The next chapter is about practically engaging the race of life. The need to run the race we have discovered.

INTERACTIVE SESSION

Chapter 2: Know Your Race

1. Do you believe that to live a better life requires you knowing your purpose of existence?

   _____
   _____
   _____
   _____
   _____
   _____
   _____
   _____

2. What is your take about this statement: "Those who truly understand their race, will equally have a good knowledge of the requirements of running the race effectively"?

   _____
   _____
   _____
   _____
   _____
   _____
   _____
   _____

3. Mention some ways through which one can discover his or her purpose of existence in life?

   _____
   _____

4. What are the advantages of knowing one's purpose or race in life?

Chapter 3
RUN YOUR RACE

"If you believe in destiny, then you know that you have a purpose.
You know things happen for a reason, and that you should find out how to live up to that essence of what you're supposed to do and which direction you are determined to take."
– V. Noot

Some years ago, someone shared with me a touching true life experience of his encounter with an elderly and successful pastor. This young pastor who shared his experience always admired how God has given so much success to this elderly minister. He envied his success stories and wished they happened to him. To him, it seems God is partial, why should it be that only this man would have such a great success in those areas. Secondly, he felt God is unkind to him after several sessions of prayer and fasting and still no substantial increase like this elderly pastor.

After much contemplation the young pastor decided to visit the elderly successful minister. He vented his frustration and expressed his desire for such success too. The elderly pastor was calm and patiently heard all he had to say. After probing into various ways through which he handled his ministry the elderly pastor said,

"Work on your calling, what you don't work does not work". We must actively and intentionally engage all necessary platforms of our race, destiny, dreams and aspirations before we can see expected growth. Jesus Christ said it so well, "My Father is always at his work to this very day, and I too am working." (John 5:17 NIV).

Previously, we had established that there is a race set before us. Another way to make it clearer is that we all have a race of destiny to run. We have a general race to run as Christians but there also is a specific race as well. The general race here implies our faith journey, the Christian race as it is commonly called. This race began the day we give our lives to Jesus Christ through the salvation of our soul. The end of the race is when we shall appear before the throne of the Master for welcome and appropriate reward.

"… For we will all stand before God's judgment seat." (Rom. 14:10 NIV).

"For we must all appear before the judgment seat of Christ, so that each of us may receive what is due us for the things done while in the body, whether good or bad." (II Cor. 5:10 NIV).

These two Bible references are few out of so many affirming to us that there is an end and there is a reward for believing and accepting Jesus Christ and for walking in His ways. Bruce Wilkinson in A Life God Rewards, succinctly puts it that our belief will determine our destination while our behaviour will determine our reward in eternity.

God in His ultimate wisdom has created us in so many unique ways with unique abilities and opportunities. These facilities informed how we have been shaped differently and given unique assignments in life. This unique assignment is sometimes called destiny or purpose. True fulfilment takes place when individuals discover their unique purpose or destiny.

It is popularly said that when purpose is not known abuse becomes inevitable. Many people live wrongly because they are partially aware of the purpose of their existence while countless multitude are completely oblivious of their assignments in life.

We are tempted often to like and sometimes prefer the grace and gifting of others. We wish we could be like them. We struggle a lot to emulate and be like them, but we end up in frustration and unfulfillment at the end of the day. Engaging in envy, snuffing off the light of others for yours to shine, backstabbing and throwing up tantrums will not help you to end with desired joy. We are warned not to be a busybody in someone's affairs, "But none of you should ever merit suffering like those who have murdered or stolen, meddled in the affairs of others or done evil things." (I Pet. 4:15 The Voice). Why get angry that others are running their destiny? Why not focus on yours?

Jesus Christ while here, worked out His assignments in life and became successful in the measure of God. "I have testimony weightier than that of John. For the works that the Father has given me to finish—the very works that I am doing —testify that the Father has sent me." (John 5:36 NIV). Jesus ran His race by working on the assignment God gave Him. To become truly successful in life and please the Lord we must run our race (I Cor. 9:24) and work out our God-given purpose (Phil. 2:12). Faithfulness is also key with God and the assignment as we run this life race (Luke 19:17). Wise people get occupied while they await the coming back of the Master (Luke 19:13).

"No food for lazy man" is street version of II Thessalonians 3:10. This expression is about building the culture of diligence in people, especially the young ones. It is good to run purposefully the race of life. It is much better to be wise to remove possible impediment on the path of one's victory. The fourth chapter concentrates on identifying those obstacles to winning the race of life.

INTERACTIVE SESSION

Chapter 3
Run Your Race

1. "We are tempted often to like and sometimes prefer the grace and gifting of others. We wish we could be like them."

   a. Why do you think people fall into this kind of temptation?

   _____
   _____
   _____
   _____
   _____

   b. What are the dangers in living like someone else?

   _____
   _____
   _____
   _____
   _____

   c. Have you been tempted to be doing like someone you so much appreciate before?

   _____
   _____
   _____
   _____

_____
_____

    d. How can you be free from this kind of temptation?

_____
_____
_____
_____

2. Do you think being a Christian waiting for the coming of Jesus should limit us from fulfilling our life purpose?

_____
_____
_____
_____
_____
_____
_____

3. Why do you think many Christians claimed to be heavenly focused and become not so fulfilled on earth?

_____
_____
_____
_____
_____

Chapter 4
WIN YOUR RACE

"It is important to understand the objective of every race. Sometimes it is important to win. Sometimes it is more than enough if you just complete the race."
— Abhishek Ratna

We have been able to establish that to end the race with joy we must first know or understand the race we are in and its nature. Also, we have discussed the need to run the race, or work on our life purpose or destiny assignment. After all, what is the essence of discovering a race or purpose you are not ready to fulfil or work on? For this section of our discourse, we shall examine qualities that are expedient in winning the race and ending with joy.

   a. Discover and Enrol in the Race. We have general Christian race also we have specific destiny race. Both should be run well. Close fellowship with Jesus and diligence in career and calling is a necessity to ending with joy. To know your race and run it is the best decision in life. (John 3:3; John 15:4 -7; I Cor. 9:27; Prov. 22:29).

b. Engage in a Profitable Relationship through Fellowship for spiritual and emotional nourishment; accountability group for focus and integrity building; mentorship to facilitate personal growth and development and through discipleship to become like Christ. (Pro. 11:14; 15:22; 24:6; Heb. 10:25; 3:13, Acts 2:42; Matthew 10:38; Mark 10:21).

c. Resist to be Conformed to the Lifestyle of the World. The rat race culture of this world will deprive one of love for God, authentic joy and shift one's focus from what really matters. Pursuing shadows will make one not to end with joy. (Romans 12:2; John 15:19; I John 2:15).

d. Don't be Overcome by Evil. Be focused and mind your life and assignment. Avoid the evil of busybody lifestyle and competitive spirit. Mind your business and compete with yourself and not with your neighbour. (I Pet. 4:15; II Cor. 10:12).

e. Never Yield to Discouragement. We are told that it is going to get tougher as the second coming of Jesus Christ draws near. Many will even get discouraged and drop out of the race. "So do not throw away your confidence; it will be richly rewarded." (Hebr. 10:35 cf. Matt. 24:12)

Whether the race of life or that of destiny, no race is easily won. It takes a lot of discipline, understanding and tenacity to run and win joyfully. The race is not for the lazy hearted. Wise people who won their races in life made a great push and sometimes at their breaking points, they still push. There is great joy that accomplishes successful push.

INTERACTIVE SESSION

Chapter 4: Win Your Race

1. Can you mention some qualities that can help one to win life race successfully?

   _____

   _____

   _____

   _____

   _____

   _____

   _____

   _____

2. How can good relationship aid to achieve purpose fulfilment in life?

   _____

   _____

   _____

   _____

   _____

   _____

3. Distraction is powerful, share some ways distraction can truncate one's life purpose from being successful?

4. Can you identify some of those things that are disturbing you from achieving the purpose you so much desired?

   d. _____

   e. _____

   f. _____

g. _____
   _____

Chapter 5
End Your Race Well

So far so good, it is apparent that those who end with joy are those who take it upon themselves to run the race seriously. The beginning point of any successful race is to define what you are cut out for and in for, know your race. The beauty of knowing your race, is to give it a push. Nothing moves until complementary energy is exerted. The cost may be enormous, yet it worth the efforts. Understand your track in life. We can now take some reflections as we conclude this discussion on winning the race with joy.

There is a section usually set aside for application in my denomination's Sunday School manual lesson some years ago. At the end of the lesson for the day we used to have a section designated as "Take Home Lessons". The Yoruba version gives me a deeper meaning, "Ẹko_ti aridimu fun lilo". This can be translated as drawn-out lessons for application. The import of that is that, after all said and done, what lesson do we have to act on? Similarly, our conclusion here carries same intent. These reflections are some of the salient points that we have discussed along the line. It is of paramount importance that these points are raised and well pondered on to drive home well the message of this book.

    a. *The race set before us is a designed assignment that is unique to every individual. Every believer is set to run his or her race.*

    God has a particular reason and purpose for creating you. Whether you are in the secular ministry or church ministry it doesn't matter. Where you are should be your assignment point. Let the Kingdom of God be advanced where you are. That is your ministry point. Give your best there.

    b. *This race carries both immediate and eternal consequences on both the believers and others he or she is commissioned to bless or minister to.*

    Ministry, calling, purpose or whatever you may use to describe the expression of your existence, be assured that it has present and future rewards. God expects you to add value to humanity. The greatest value you can add is to see a soul come to Christ and nurtured and prepared for eternity. Other values have to do with providing, material support, ministering growth through discipleship, career mentoring and other related human needs.

c. *This race involves serious challenges that may be sometimes unpalatable, yet the race must be carried out and ended well.*

Nothing of worth is cheap. Kingdom business is a serious business and its price is inestimable. Following Jesus is not expected to be easy. If Jesus could suffer such a great ordeal we are to be prepared for same if not more. Never lose heart because of your present pains here on earth. Strive to make it to heaven and you will have a better gain for all your troubles. God does not lie. He will pay back big time.

d. *This race has embedded guiding rules that every "runner" (believer) must be acquainted with and run according to the rules of engagement.*

The race is not a careless or carefree type, if it is, it does not worth the pains. It is wisdom to know the rules behind your race. The rules of the game are simple and clearly stated in the Word of God. It will be a great jeopardy to run the race based on popular opinion or by what is trendy.

e. *This race calls for you to be resolute with your decision to run and finish your race well.*

According to Acts 20:22-23, it becomes clear to us that Paul despite severe pains awaiting him in Jerusalem was resolute to face it because he wanted to complete the task and end well. Every believer must ask for the grace to finish his/her race with joy.

There is great joy when we finish well. Paul painted for us the ecstatic animation of having a great ending: "I have fought the good fight, I have finished the race, I have kept the faith. Now there is in store for me the crown of righteousness, which the Lord, the righteous Judge, will award to me on that day —and not only to me, but also to all who have longed for his appearing."

(II Tim. 4:7-8 NIV). What a pleasant and fulfilling height to attain?

May we all be empowered through God's unfailing grace to run well and finish with joy and fulfilment our race in life, Amen!

INTERACTIVE SESSION

Chapter 5: End Your Race Well

1. Can you write down in clear terms what you believe you exist for as a person?

   _____
   _____
   _____
   _____
   _____
   _____
   _____
   _____

_____

_____

2. Can you mention what you will like people to know you for after you might have gone?

_____

_____

_____

_____

_____

_____

_____

_____

3. Mention 5 practical things you want to begin to do to fulfil your race in life and eternity?

    a. _____

    _____

    b. _____

    _____

    c. _____

    _____

d. _____
   _____

e. _____
   _____

Printed in Great Britain
by Amazon